Love Poems

by

Purple Ronnie

First published 1994 by Statics (London) Ltd.

This edition published 2000 by Boxtree
an imprint of Macmillan Publishers Ltd
25 Eccleston Place London SW1W 9NF
Basingstoke and Oxford

www.macmillian.co.uk

Associated companies throughout the world

ISBN 0 7522 7147 4

9 8 7 6 5 4

A CIP catalogue record for this book is available from
the British Library.

Text by Giles Andreae
Illustrations by Janet Cronin and Giles Andreae
Additional material by Simon Andreae
Printed and bound in Great Britain by The Bath Press, Bath

To my mates

Nev, Maisie, Gordon and Shirlee

Contents

loads of
soppy love poems
by <u>me</u>

a poem about

↓

Loving You

How many ways do I love you?
I think there are probably two
The rumpety-pump way
Is all very well
But I like the soppy way too

Kissing

Some kisses last for just seconds

They're gentle and go on the cheeks

But I like the ones you put
right on the lips

That can go on for 2 or 3 weeks

Smashing Mate

You're chocolate cake
and soft ice-cream
Piled high upon my plate
You're a double jelly
Sandwich dream
My splendid smashing mate

a poem to say

I Love You

Sometimes when it's late at night
And we're alone together
I want to take you in my arms
And cuddle you for ever

Love

Love,
When we're <u>SNOGGING</u>
I'd like to crumble
Biscuits in your hair

Friends

Some people think that it's great
to be rich
To be cool and keep up with the
trends
But riches and looks just don't
matter at all
Cos what really counts is your friends

no cash →

smashing mates →

← Nev's latest tie

a poem about ↓

Sex Maniacs

They dream about sex every hour
of the day
They dream when they work
And they dream when they play
They dream about sex in the bath
and in bed
They never get naughty thoughts
out of their head

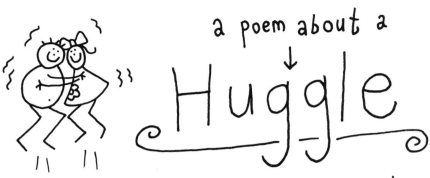

a poem about a

Huggle

A huggle is something you share
with a friend

You can huggle in all kinds of ways

Huggling makes you feel all sort
of warm

And perfectly splendid for days

us after
a good
huggle

a poem for a

Gorgeously Smashing Person

However much money I pay people

Some of them still won't agree

That you're almost as

wonderfully scrumptious

And gorgeously smashing as me

mirror

us looking gorgeously smashing

How to Be a Boyfriend

Sometimes you've got to be macho
And do lots of things that are tough
But sometimes it's best to be quiet and gentle
And say loads of soppy type stuff

whisper

It's good to have hundreds of muscles
And girls always like a nice bum
But you mustn't be hairy or sweaty
or fat
Or have any flab on your tum

Don't ever talk about football
Or make nasty smells in the bed
Or joke about bosoms with mates in
                              the pub
Or drink till you're out of your head

You've got to be funny and clever
And do loads of things by surprise
Like shouting out loud in the back of
                              the bus
"My girlfriend's got beautiful eyes!"

You don't need to have too much money
But make sure you've just got enough
To buy loads of presents and chocolates
                                    and flowers
And sexy silk undies and stuff

Say to your girlfriend "you're gorgeous
Your body's a twelve out of ten
You're sexy and beautiful, clever and kind"
Then tell her all over again

a poem about ↓

Missing You

There are times when I really
do miss you
And think of you missing me too
So I close my eyes tight
And I daydream
That I am together with you

Snogging

true love

It's funny how us people
Show our love by touching tongues

But at least we're not all doggies

Or we'd sniff each others <u>bums!</u>

sniff
sniff

down
boy!

My Lover

I'd like to tell you something
I hope it won't offend
But if you weren't my lover
You'd be my bestest friend

us wearing
saucy
undies →

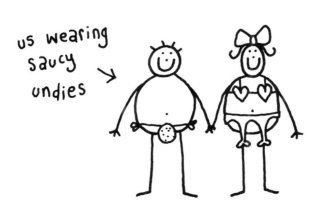

a recipe for
↓
Love Pie

by Purple Ronnie

Take a pint of tickle juice
And whisk it till it's thick
Pick a crop of cuddle fruit
And crush them with a stick

hee hee hee hee

Nibble eighteen earlobes
As gently as you can
Then grate a little botty kiss
And put it in the pan

Dip a snog in snuggle sauce
And let it rest a while
Then soak it in hug marinade
And season with a smile

Add a pinch of happy spice
Grown in huggle town
And bake it in the oven
Till it comes out golden brown

a poem about

cuddling

I NEED A CUDDLE

I sometimes have feelings
You don't understand
That make me confused and befuddled
So don't go to sleep
When you turn out the light
Cos sometimes I like to be cuddled

a poem for a
↓

Loving Person

Loving people like to give
Their love to everyone
That's why Loving People's love
Is so much lovely fun

a shy poem
↓
To Someone I Like

I sometimes find it rather hard

To say I really care

And that I like you quite a lot

But I've said it now-so there

hot
flush

Safe Sex

To make sure you're safe when you DO IT
Put on a Thingie that fits
I like the ones that can glow in the dark
With the slippery nobbly bits

Men

Some men I know
Make love into an art
And always keep going
Till morning
But others I know
Just roll over and fart
When they've finished the job
Then start snoring

Love Poem

I just want to tell you
I love you so much
That each time I look at your face
My heart jumps a somersault
Round in the air
And my feelings explode into space

a poem about feeling

Smiley Inside

<u>Lov</u>e makes you feel all cuddly
and warm

Love makes your tongue get all tied

It makes you go wobbly

And weak at the knees

And all sort of smiley inside

I Like You

You tell me I'm fat and I'm ugly
You tell me I'm utterly nuts
You tell me I burp and I fart
and I smell
But that's why I like you so
much

Doing It

Who first thought of doing
What it is you're meant to do?
I'm glad he was so brainy
I'd have never guessed would you?

a poem for a

Lover

If someone invented a gadget

That made me terrific in bed

I think I'd buy twenty-five thousand

And Do It with you till I'm dead

a poem to say

I Love You

When I am lying alone in my bed
All sorts of thoughts come into my head
Like why do I Love You as much as I do?
Then I know it's because you are <u>You</u>

My Own Little Way

I sometimes get rather embarrassed
And don't always know what to say
When it comes to expressing my
feelings
But I try in my own little way

Friendly Poem

Never think twice about calling
me up
To say that your pride has been
dented
To tell me you're happy or lonely
or sad
Cos that is why friends were
invented

...you'd never guess...he... ...and then...he...

she never!

brilliant invention ←

a poem about

Men I Like

I like men who talk
About interesting things
Like music and science and art
But most men I know
When they've had a few drinks
Just talk about sex and then fart

Love Poem

Crikey I love you to pieces
My heart wants to jump up and shout
Let's walk through the flowers
And huggle for hours
And let all our loveliness out

Snuggle Pie

You to me are everything
That money just can't buy
Like creamy cuddle custard
And scrumptious snuggle pie

custard love
↓

a poem for an

Extra Special Friend

If I had a million pounds
I know what I would do
I'd buy some extra special times
And spend them all with you

Hugging Poem

I want you to know
That I think you are great
And although I'm a bit of a mug
If you ever need me
I'll always be near
To come round and give you a
hug

squeeze

feeling → better

Being in Love

thumpety
thump

Whenever I'm with you
My heart starts to thump
And I come over wonky and flustered
I try to stay calm
But pour milk on my toast
And butter my coffee with mustard

← me so
in love

MILK

a poem for a
↓

BOYFRIEND

You're a hunky handsome
heart-throb
You're a fab and groovy dude
You're a juicy lump of
gorgeousness
A scrumptious plate of food

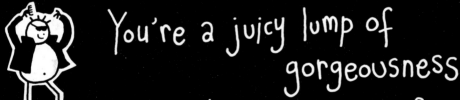

You're a hot and horny lover
And if I had my way 
I would smother you
in chocolate
And feast on you all day

Loving

Loving a person is easy
If only you've got the right knack
— It's heaping your happiness
All over someone
Who loves heaping happiness back

Love Bank

I wish there was a Love Bank
Where we all had big accounts
And we'd pay for things with kisses
And give snogs for large amounts

what is Love?

It must be sort of squidgey
Like a bouncy rubber ball
Cos I know that when you fall
                        in it
It doesn't hurt at all

I know that people make it
But they never tell me where
And I think that there's a funny tribe
Who rub it in their hair

love
dance

piece
of
love

I wonder what
it looks like
I've heard it's splendid stuff
I suppose it's sort of furry
Like my tummy button fluff

Also by Purple Ronnie

Purple Ronnie's History of the World

☆

Purple Ronnie's Little Guide to Boyfriends

☆

Purple Ronnie's Little Poems for Friends

☆

Purple Ronnie's Little Guide for Lovers

☆

Purple Ronnie's Little Book of Willies and Bottoms